IS CHRISTIANITY JUST FIRE INSURANCE?

# CHASING HEAVEN TO AVOID HELL

IS CHRISTIANITY JUST FIRE INSURANCE?

# CHASING HEAVEN TO AVOID HELL

## Jean Sheldon

**Pacific Press Publishing Association**
Boise, Idaho
Montemorelos, Nuevo Leon, Mexico
Oshawa, Ontario, Canada

Unless otherwise noted, all Bible texts in this book are from the King James Version.

Bible texts credited to T.E.V. are from the *Good News Bible*—Old Testament: Copyright © American Bible Society 1976; New Testament: Copyright © American Bible Society 1966, 1971, 1976.

Scripture quotations marked R.S.V. are from the *Revised Standard Version of the Bible*, copyrighted 1946, 1952 © 1971, 1973.

Texts credited to N.I.V. are from *The Holy Bible: New International Version*. Copyright © 1978 by the New York International Bible Society. Used by permission of Zondervan Bible Publishers.

Texts credited to N.E.B. are from *The New English Bible,* © The Delegates of the Oxford University Press and the Syndics of the Cambridge University Press 1961, 1970. Reprinted by permission.

Scripture quotations marked N.K.J.V. are from *The Holy Bible, New King James Version*, copyright © 1979, 1980, 1982 by Thomas Nelson, Inc. Used by permission.

Designed by Tim Larson
Cover photos by NASA, Nona Guerriere, Duane Tank

Copyright © 1985 by
Pacific Press Publishing Association
Printed in United States of America
All Rights Reserved

**Library of Congress Cataloging in Publication Data**

Sheldon, Jean, 1956—
   Chasing heaven to avoid hell.

   1. Christian life—Seventh-Day Adventist authors. 2. Salvation. I. Title.
BV4501.2.S4366    1985    230'.6372    85-3462
ISBN 0-8163-0600-1

85 86 87 88 89 • 6 5 4 3 2 1

# Preface

If you already bask in the assurance that you have salvation, you may not wish to read on. That is fine. This book is for those who are struggling to find peace with God, but for whom the usual, even most attractive, ways to do so have failed to bring them assurance.

Many of us wish for answers to our quest for eternal life, a faith which makes sense, and a religion which fits together into a consistent whole. It is to help supply these tangible needs that I have written the following pages.

If you have hidden anywhere inside your mind a secret fear about the judgment, God, salvation, or hell, read on. You should find your fears greatly relieved and be enabled to face the Eternal One in absolute trust.

# Contents

1. Do You have the Assurance of Salvation? 9
2. Ways We Find Security 12
3. The Ticket Plan 16
4. Does the Blood Do It? 20
5. Get-a-way From Hell 23
6. What Started This Need for Assurance? 26
7. Why Doesn't He Do Something? 32
8. The Truth Will Set You Free 36
9. The God of the Bible 40
10. Assurance Before God's Judgment Bar 45
11. A Swordless God 53
12. Coming to Know God 59

*Chapter 1*

# Do You Have the Assurance of Salvation?

"If Jesus were to come tonight, would you have the assurance that you would be saved?" The question, tossed out solicitously to a group of academy seniors by the Bible teacher, hit my ears like the clanging of metal against metal. As an eighteen-year-old attending a church-operated school, I had been firmly taught that Jesus was coming soon. And I believed it. But the question raised some issues that I hadn't considered before. In one way I wasn't sure why I didn't like it. In another way, I *knew*. It raised the hidden dragons of my subconscious fears: What if I were unready?

"I don't think that is a very good question," I countered bluntly.

"Why not?" our Bible teacher asked. (Fortunately for me, he believed in giving his students the freedom to disagree with him!)

"It's too hypothetical," I replied. "We know that certain things must take place before Jesus can come, and they haven't. Obviously He isn't going to come *tonight*."

Unfortunately, my classmates agreed with me, so the teacher rephrased his question. While I tended to agree that his second attempt was better than his first, I still fought inwardly over the need for assurance. Hadn't I been taught that it was presumptuous to claim assurance?

Yet I felt a need of assurance. Should I *not* have that assurance of salvation? If so, on what basis? Did I need that assurance in order to be saved? If I did, why? But beyond all these questions, one stood out: If I didn't have that assurance, how would I go about getting it?

My Christian experience so far had not been unique—I had discovered this from listening to and reading about the experiences of others. I had my ups and downs, just as they did. Some nights I felt as though I were a totally rotten sinner. Other times, as I reflected on the kind of person God is, my worries vanished and I felt secure. If I was a normal beginning Christian, I reflected, did I need to be concerned that I had assurance of eternal life?

For a while I pondered the teacher's question with its implications. For a while I worried about having the assurance of salvation—as if that were a requirement for getting into heaven. But the burden became a little too heavy. So I went back to my normal relationship with God in which I focused on knowing Him instead of on my status with Him.

As a result, my fears of whether or not I would be saved greatly lessened.

## But I Need Assurance!

Nearly every Christian who is determined to be saved has found—or is finding—a way to have the assurance that he or she is saved. Now, having made such a bold statement, let me hasten to add that the way of finding assurance may not bring genuine assurance. It may only add to the anxiety of the possibility of condemnation. It may weigh one down with heavy burdens and increase the strain of life's stresses. But to the person who has found a particular means of assurance, it is the *only* way to be secure.

When someone finds a method or reason to feel secure,

## DO YOU HAVE THE ASSURANCE OF SALVATION?

he usually is very quick to share the same method or reason with others so that they too can find "peace with God."

At one level, this is only appropriate. Why shouldn't we share the good news of our assurance? Why shouldn't we want everyone to have a similar security in knowing they will enjoy eternal life? But a straightforward, deeper look reveals some hazards.

If Mrs. Bower, for example, believes that memorizing Scripture is going to make her ready for heaven, she will probably not be content with sharing merely the joys of memorizing the Bible. Most likely she will tell her friend Anne Palmer that she had better start memorizing at least one verse a day, or she will never "make it"! In fear, Anne may start memorizing, but she will probably not obtain the great relief Mrs. Bower has that she is therefore on the right road to heaven.

Mrs. Bower may not really be sharing her security of eternal life with Anne Palmer; she may unwittingly be trying to foist on her the *means* of her own assurance. In other words, Mrs. Bower may unconsciously be trying to gain assurance that her method of obtaining the assurance of salvation is valid!

Why do we have this intense desire to find security that all is well between us and God? What can this great desire lead us to do? What bases for assurance have some people found? Let's look at a few of these.

Chapter 2

# Ways We Find Security

**Rules Make You a Jewel**

Did you ever sing this song as a child?

> Jesus wants me for a sunbeam
> To shine for Him each day.
> In every way try to please Him
> At home, at school, at play.

It's cute to watch little tots waving big yellow streamers while they sing this song. But the idea enters firmly into their wee minds very quickly: Someday Jesus will come, and those boys and girls who have been real good and have obeyed their mommies and daddies (and anyone else who prescribes rules) will be His sunbeams. So if you want to be one of Jesus' sunbeams, BE REAL GOOD!

How well I remember that method of trying to gain assurance that Jesus wouldn't frown at me when He came! At age seven it was my duty to dust the upstairs once a week. The job took me much longer than necessary due to my fear that if I "missed that corner" Jesus wouldn't save me. Just where I got that "rule" I'm not sure, but it seemed to have something to do with the story of Booker

T. Washington who dusted and swept a room three or four times to satisfy a prospective boss.

At any rate, if keeping the rules was the means of getting to heaven, I was determined to keep each one. And since I found it fairly easy to be obedient, I found great assurance that I would be saved. I also made the lives of those around me rather troublesome by my pharisaic attitude. That didn't bother me, though; I figured that that was their problem. All I knew was that my being good got me in good favor with God.

**Health Brings God's Great Wealth**

A few years back, some of my college friends became great enthusiasts about living healthfully. Certain foods became taboo: milk and milk products, oil, all refined products, etc. A lot of discussion took place about fresh air, exercise, and water. Not that these items are bad in themselves. But if I wanted to feel unwanted or alienated, all I needed to do was to walk by their table in the cafeteria with milk on my tray or even to bring up what I had found to be good news about God. Living healthfully seemed, at times, to be the primary item on their agenda of salvation.

And yet, remembering my own past, I could sense where they were coming from. My own thoughts had wandered down a few similar alleys at one time: "Let's see, if I really eat this yucky food (without salt), run every morning, avoid milk, eggs, yogurt, cheese, oil—have I left out anything?—I'll be able to gain something with God!"

A lot of people today (and in ancient times) feel very secure with God because they are healthy. When a person's health fails, his religious experience is often questioned. After all, the idea goes: God blesses those who are in His favor with health.

Many years ago, a man named Job faced this problem. After losing everything he owned through "natural" disasters—flocks, herds, sons, daughters, and servants, he became seriously ill. And in the land and era of Job, it was a foregone conclusion that health and wealth equaled God's favor and that the absence of these two meant that you were a terrible sinner suffering from His wrath. Three friends came to comfort Job and to plead with him to repent from the sins that were causing his suffering. But Job wasn't most worried about his sins, nor the loss of his wealth, nor the enormous ache in his heart at the memory of a recent mass funeral. He wasn't even so concerned about his status with God. What Job cried out most bitterly about was the fact that at the moment God seemed so far away and silent. Their former very close relationship was broken. Like the Lord in whom he trusted, Job cried out from his cross, "My God, my God, why have You forsaken me?"

To Job's three friends, health and wealth were their assurance of acceptance with God. To Job, it was to be God's friend. When God gave the last word on Job, He didn't commend him for his courage or his righteous works. Rather, he announced that Job had spoken "the truth about me." See Job 42:7, 8, TEV.

## Get on the Right Plane

Have you ever bought an airline ticket, settled down at the right time on the plane, fastened your seatbelt for the take-off, felt the power surge through the engines as the plane lifted from the runway—and suddenly discovered you were on the wrong plane?

Fortunately, I haven't. But one night I nearly lost my ticket at a very large international airport. After dashing frantically down one terminal and back, I actually became afraid that I might be standing in the wrong line heading

for the wrong destination. "This plane is going to Los Angeles, isn't it?" I asked the attendant at the door.
It was. In fact, just after I was seated safely in my assigned seat, I heard the pilot announce: "Ladies and Gentlemen, this is flight number 182 headed for LA International Airport. If you are on the wrong plane, please get off immediately. This is your last chance!"

Somehow I had to smile in smug security.

Many people feel the same way about getting to heaven as I felt about getting to Los Angeles that night. Just get on the right plane, and you'll be OK. Just belong to the right church, and you'll be saved.

Yet a great many people got on the right plane heading for Los Angeles from O'Hare one fateful Friday in May 1979, who never reached their destination.

What if the plane isn't "safe"? Or even if the plane is safe, will all aboard it arrive safely? Is salvation a "church" matter? Or a personal matter? Is one's destination determined by his relationship with the church? Or by his relationship with God?

A couple of young people knocked on my door recently with a message from their church which strongly believes in witnessing. Their opening question surprised me a little: "Suppose your church fell apart," they asked. "Would you still trust God?"

"Yes," I replied, "my faith is not in a church but in a Person—God."

Paul didn't boast of the fact that he was a Jew. He didn't boast that he was a Christian. He didn't boast that he was a member of God's family. His boast took this slant: "I take pride in the good news; it is God's power to save everyone who trusts in Him because in it is revealed God's own righteousness." See Romans 1:16, 17; Philippians 3:2-11.

*Chapter 3*

# The Ticket Plan

The most popular means of obtaining the assurance of eternal life is to look at the cross as the full and complete statement of salvation. Brad put it this way: "Jesus' blood shed on the cross paid for my sins and freed me from my load of guilt." Gary added to the same idea: "I never really had assurance until I accepted that fact."

Guilt versus acquittal is the emphasis. Certainly all of us have felt guilty. Deep down at the nadir of our minds we are very aware of that gnawing emptiness and insecurity that something is not quite right with our world, and even further, that something is very wrong with us. We sense we are headed for some kind of terrible destruction. And every time we sin, we stack up another cement block of guilt to enclose ourselves away from God.

What is that guilt and how do we get rid of it? Are we guilty only because God has said we are? Are the sins which make us feel guilty sins only because someone has said that God has so declared them to be?

Many believe that the real problem of sin is the problem of guilt and the record of our sins. This is why Jesus' death has such legal significance for the majority of Christians. "By means of the cross," I've heard many say, "Jesus paid the penalty for our sins and removed our guilt, and thus God's justice has been satisfied. Now God can declare those who accept this payment as righteous."

But is this enough to do away with our guilt? Does it do away with our guilt to know that because of our guilt, Jesus, the innocent Son of God, died such a horrible death? How can merely knowing that we are guilty of Jesus' death free us from guilt?

And how can we know that when God declares us to be righteous that His declaration is enough? Is a mere statement a fact? Can God be trusted to follow through with His promise to forgive and justify us? On what basis?

A lot of Christians are sitting at the airport with their tickets stamped "paid at the cross" waiting for Jesus to come. How do they know their tickets will be accepted at the gate when their flight number is called? And even if their tickets are accepted, how do they know that the pilot will give them a safe journey home? Do they know for sure that their stay with Jesus and the Father will be pleasant?

Perhaps this is knowledge we should assume. Or maybe it isn't right to ask such questions. But can we—should we—trust Someone we do not know? Merely on someone else's say-so? Can faith in God be genuine without evidence that He is trustworthy?

Perhaps our most important question for the moment is, Do the same tickets which seem to guarantee us a seat on the plane to eternal life guarantee the evidence that God can be trusted?

## Lost Ticket and Boarding Time

Several years ago, I traveled from southwestern Michigan to Los Angeles, thanks to a ticket my father bought for me. At the South Bend, Indiana, airport, I faced some hassles over its validity which nearly prevented me from reaching O'Hare airport on time and thus making the proper connections. But at last I arrived in Chicago, relieved that all was going well.

My stomach reminded me that I was two hours late in giving it something, so I looked for a place to eat my lunch. Wishing to remain inconspicuous, I chose the most quiet restaurant I could find and sat down in a far corner. I had barely pulled out a carrot stick, when a waitress told me that I couldn't eat there. Going to a sandwich shop, I asked a waitress if I could eat there. Permission granted, I sat down, pulled out a sandwich—only to be informed by another waitress that health regulations ruled out eating my own lunch in any airport restaurant.

Picking up my carry-on baggage, I trudged to gate 12, the last gate in the terminal, where I was to board my plane. One glance at the waiting room told me that everybody and his great-uncle was heading for southern California; every seat held an occupant. Resigned, I sat on the floor, pulled out my carrot stick and began munching.

Suddenly a nasty little thought lit up a question mark in my weary mind. "Do I have my ticket?" I looked in my lunch sack. No ticket. Frantically, I searched my overnight case. No ticket. The question mark became an ugly black exclamation point to emphasize that my ticket was almost anywhere within the block. And I had less than fifteen minutes left until boarding time!

Leaving my baggage in care of a very kind attendant, I rushed back down the terminal, scanning the floor. No ticket. At the check stop, I asked the attendants if they had seen my ticket. They began pulling apart the conveyer belt and said they would page me if they found it. I raced on to the sandwich shop; but my ticket was not there. That left only the restaurant I'd entered first.

Into that place I ran, and, finding the nearest waitress, I asked if she'd seen a ticket.

"No," she said, "I'm sorry but I haven't."

In despair I turned, prepared to run back to the ticket

booth and request another ticket, when the waitress who had ordered me out said, "I found your ticket!"

Running back to Gate 12, I puffed up to the line just beginning to move into the plane!

Obviously, the fact that my ticket was paid for did not guarantee that I would reach Los Angeles.

What can guarantee us that we will reach heaven? Is the cross our ticket? Is healthful living our assurance? Is the right church the means of transportation?

More important, can we know that when we arrive we will feel comfortable with the Father who comes to pick us up at the airport?

*Chapter 4*

# Does the Blood Do It?

Since the time we first learned that "there is a heaven to win and a hell to shun" we have frantically searched for some means to know that we have won and shunned the appropriate places! Unfortunately, getting that assurance is perhaps not as easy as accepting a free trip to Hawaii.

As we grow older and learn more about the place called heaven and the one called hell, we become increasingly aware that God is the only One with the keys to both (or so we are taught), for He decides our future fate. Therefore, if we can obtain His favor, we have it made. If we can't, He will make sure that we receive the appropriate and adequate punishment we deserve.

Consequently, we become preoccupied with one primary aim: to get in good with God.

As we have seen, the ways people contrive to "get in good" with God are innumerable (we discussed a mere sampling). Even holding up Christ's blood on the cross is an attempt to win God's favor, to get Him to be on our side. Of course, this last method is favorable to most of us because it relieves us of our futile struggles to produce God's smile through "being good" or whatever else we contrive. Instead of our own sweat and blood we can present Christ's sweat and blood and thus gain something with God.

Yet even this formula presupposes that the sin problem is not primarily man's problem, but is actually God's problem. If we could just twist His arm (or believe that He has twisted His own arm), all will be well. If His anger can be vented once and for all on a victim, thus demonstrating His vindictive justice against sin, then He will be able to forgive us poor sinners who cannot possibly satisfy His strict commands anyway.

For centuries, millions on this planet have struggled to gain the favor of the gods through the shedding of blood. Perverting the sacrificial system of the Old Testament, they conceived that deity must be appeased. From the slicing of animal jugular veins to the bathing of one's body in a fountain of blood to the burning of innocent babies—all this was done to "get in good" with God.

Of course, our sensitive, cultured Christianity gapes in horror at such practices. How heathenish and vile, we shudder!

Yet millions of Christians in all communions have stood in imagination at the foot of the cross and praised God for venting His wrath on His Son that they might have eternal life. For if the sin problem demands that God kills sinners and Jesus is the sinner's substitution, the vicarious Atonement who died for him, then God must have killed His Son as He would have killed human beings had He not chosen grace and forgiveness.

So, in the place of the blood of bulls and goats we have the blood of One who "went about doing good, and healing all who were oppressed of the devil." Acts 10:38.

In place of the screams of innocent babies, we have the cry of a thirty-three-year-old Man.

And in the place of a blood-thirsty Moloch, we have a blood-demanding Judge who raises the sword of justice over the head of His "beloved" Son.

If we do not love this God enough to accept the ticket paid for with His Son's blood, which guarantees us a place on the plane home, He will raise the sword of justice over our heads, and it will be our blood and our screams of pain that will be heard.

Of course, if we accept the ticket, we will live—forever and ever—with the same blood-demanding Judge!

I've been told it's easy to accept the ticket. All you have to do is to accept Jesus' death on the cross and believe in Him as Lord. If you do this you will be saved—but if you don't you will burn in hell.

Somehow I'm not so sure it's that easy. Would living near a Judge who threatened me with torture if I didn't love Him, who killed His Son on a cross to show me how much He hated sin, who keeps my lost friends down in a place of torment—would this be enjoyable?

Is my choice really between paradise and purging flames? Or is it really a choice between a tyrant called Satan and a partial tyrant called by some God? Must I choose between a lesser of two hells?

What really does give me the assurance that I can trust and feel safe with the God who, it seems, often brandishes a two-edged sword?

Chapter 5

# Get-a-way From Hell

An eighth-grade girl studied the survey thoughtfully. Question number three read, "What is God like to you? Describe Him." "He's loving and kind," she answered, "and merciful and just." She put her hand on her chin. Was that enough? She shrugged. Well, at least that was what she had been taught.

Question number ten twisted her thoughts like a hemp rope. "Do you really want to go to heaven? Why or why not?" Why did *that* have to be on the survey? Of course she wanted to go to heaven—er, well, she *had* to want to go to heaven. It would be sinful not to want to go. But the "why or why not?" tied the knot on the end of her twisted thoughts. Her honesty smote her on this. She knew why she wanted to go to heaven. It was the only safe place to go. You see, there was that other place which hurt a great deal; and of course, she didn't want to go there.

With torn strokes of the pen, she wrote "Yes" to the question, "Do you want to go to heaven?" To the "why?" she answered, "Because I don't want to burn."

She paused before handing in the paper. Was there a better way to say it? Suddenly she felt torn between honesty and duty. She really didn't want to burn, but that shouldn't be the reason why one wanted to go to heaven. She searched her young heart further. At first there was a glimmer, then a gleam, then a glow. Yes, YES, she did want to see Jesus.

Again she bent over question number ten, "Do you want to go to heaven? Why or why not?" When she handed in her paper her answer read, "Yes, because I don't want to burn, and I want to see Jesus."

Ever since the blending of paganism with Judaism, most God-fearing saints have understood that God would burn His wicked creatures in hell for ever and ever. With fervid zeal, Christians marched across Turkey, swinging their swords and in the name of God's justice wiping out the hordes of heathen. The holy wars were "holy" because they believed God would do worse things than they to the helpless victims of sanctified justice.

The Inquisitors of the Middle Ages burned heretics at the stake and tortured them on the rack, not because they hated the heretics, but because they hoped to save their souls. After all, the slow, torturing flames of the fagot were far less to be feared than the endless agony of that turbulent sea of vengeful fire, stoked from eternity by an angry God.

During the last century, revivalist preachers stalked the land for souls to save. Their chief weapon to bring them to repentance?—vivid descriptions of human agony amid the eternal flames of God's wrath. Thousands, including my own great-grandfather, fled from this picture of God to one which left Him out altogether. After all, if one should obtain His mercy and so reach heaven, would living with such a deity really be desirable?

Which is most favorable—to escape hell and live forever with the invincible Judge who keeps hell burning or to escape living with such a person and spend eternity in . . . the same hell?

Of course there seems to be a softening down on hell in certain quarters. Maybe it's not really an ever-burning fire but rather eternal separation. Or perhaps the fire goes out and life's existence with it. If this be true, if God is waving a sword over our heads (as He once waved it over His Son) demanding, "Love Me or I'll kill you!" then perhaps the better paradise is really hell with its non-existence. How could anyone enjoy a Paradise in the presence of One who holds a threatening sword behind His back?

Is real security based merely on *where* we spend eternity? Or does our greatest assurance depend on the kind of Person with *whom* we spend it?

Or are these questions that one should not ask? Is it "none of our business" to consider the kind of God with whom we plan to spend eternity? Surely God does not demand that we serve Him with mindless trust, robotic reverence, and forced love. This would imply that God doesn't want a genuine relationship with us, but only one that exists beneath the pressure of an almighty thumb. Remove the pressure and everyone would explode into rebellion.

The question, "Do you have assurance that you have eternal life?"—let's face it; it is really a question about God. All our fears, anxieties, quests for security have grown out of our understandings or misunderstandings of what He is like.

Chapter 6

# What Started This Need for Assurance?

Separation from God is not usually one of man's chief concerns. Actually, at heart, he rather enjoys being separated from his Creator. That is, while he may at times feel fear of eternal separation from Him, he more often feels terror at the thought of meeting God face to face!

Why? Because, we often say, man knows he is a rebellious sinner and yet perceives that God is holy and undefiled. For him to meet God face to face anywhere, at any time, would seem to require a drastic change in man. God won't change, so man must. But man can't on his own. So fear comes between man and God.

But is that the only cause of fear? Does man really recognize what God's holiness is? How could he—apart from a divinely given revelation of God's character? Many throughout history have, in the name of God's holiness, tortured their opponents to death. (See John 16:2.) The God-fearing worshipers in the time of Christ scourged and crucified the great "I AM" as an act of service to their "holy" God.

They too feared God. They too worried about whether or not they would be saved. They too would have run in terror at meeting their Creator in all His radiant glory. But what they didn't realize was that their Creator had been among them during the previous thirty-three and a half years; they only knew that they hated this heretic who

## WHAT STARTED THIS NEED FOR ASSURANCE?

claimed to be God yet acted so graciously, so gently, whose holiness did not hold a sword, whose dignity delighted to kneel before His traitor and wash his dirty feet.

They preferred to be afraid of God, to be preoccupied with "getting in good" with Him, rather than to sit at His feet and listen to His gracious words about the Father.

Why does it feel good, at times, to be afraid of God? Does this, perhaps, suggest that we believe God delights in our fear? Surely He wouldn't bar Heaven's gates to someone who was afraid of Him!

Or would He?

Sometimes the fear lies so deep that we don't admit how afraid we really are of Him. If we really were honest with ourselves and our fears emerged, perhaps we would wish relief from their burden.

Why is it we are afraid of God? When and how did those fears begin?

The first biblical story recording fear is found in Genesis 3. Adam and Eve had eaten the fruit which God had requested they not eat. Suddenly they heard God walking through their garden home to visit them as He always had before in the cool of the day. Always before they had welcomed Him eagerly. Nothing had come in between them and their beloved Friend. To talk with Him was the highlight of each day.

But now the sounds that earlier had spelled to them the joy of His love seemed sinister and cruel. In terror they ran to hide.

Why? Had God changed? Did He come that evening wielding a sword of justice? Is that why they were afraid?

**Afraid of God**

Remember those nights as a small child when you peered through the darkness of your room? Suddenly you saw a big black object at your closet door. It looked as though it were moving toward your bed. What was it? A bear? An evil person? Quickly you buried your face under the covers and stifled your desire to scream.

Nothing happened, so finally you turned your face away from the "monster" and fell asleep. When the rays of the sun woke you up the next morning, you peeked over the covers to catch a glimpse of the beast that had so frightened you the night before. Relief! Hanging from the doorknob were your jeans, shirt, and jacket, just where you'd placed them the previous evening.

What made you afraid? The clothes themselves or the distortions of them which you saw in the darkness?

Fear is often based upon distortions of reality rather than upon reality itself. Such was the case with the fears of Adam and Eve in the Garden of Eden. God hadn't changed, but their perceptions of Him had.

Just shortly before their Father-Friend came to visit them that awful evening, our first parents had made the most fateful decision in earth's history. To protect them from the wily serpent lurking in the tree of knowledge of good and evil, God had warned them not to eat of its fruit. His greatest concern was not over the fruit itself but rather over the philosophy of the one who lurked among the branches of the tree. To the tree came the unsuspecting Eve, and, unfortunately, she stayed to listen.

"Oh!" the snake sneered, as if reading her mind. "Has God really said you must not eat of the trees of the garden? Sounds rather selfish to me."

"Oh no," said the surprised Eve. "God didn't say that. It's just this one tree. He said we shouldn't touch its fruit or eat of it lest we die."

"You won't die!" Scorn dripped from the serpent's voice. "The fruit won't hurt you (God might hurt you, but eating it won't)! You know, Eve, you really can't trust God to always tell the truth. Actually He has motives for making such a terrible threat. You see, He knows that

## WHAT STARTED THIS NEED FOR ASSURANCE? 29

if you eat this fruit you will become like Him, knowing good and evil. Yes, that's right, Eve, God knows evil as well as good. There is something slightly less loving about Him if you don't stay on His good side. He's really jealous lest you find out His secret and usurp His authority. At heart all He wants is your servile obedience; He wants yes-people who will dutifully do exactly as they are told without raising questions. Really, you can't trust Him to be consistent."

With clever innuendos and plausible falsehoods, the creature in the tree presented a distorted picture of Eve's gracious God. She and Adam chewed up his cunning words along with the fruit from the tree and believed them to be true. But the "wisdom" they obtained was darkness of mind and loss of rational discernment and sane reasoning.

When, through their now twisted senses, they heard God coming for His evening visit, His voice sounded like frightening music, and they ran in terror.

God had not changed, but their perception of Him had. And now they saw their friendly Creator as an enemy coming through the darkness of their minds to hurt them, hate them, perhaps destroy them.

Yet He was only on His way to try to win them back in love!

**Those First Lies**

Their heavenly Father, who now looked so grossly distorted in the darkness of Satan's lies, well knew that this was not the first time the serpent had lied about Him. Originally, the being disguised as a serpent had been one of God's most majestic, intelligent creatures, a real friend of His. The serpentine form was really only a disguise to hide the wily Lucifer.

Lucifer, son of the morning! See Isaiah 14:12. How

proud God had been of that tall, winsome angel who had joined with God's own Son to make the character of the Creator known to other angels. No created being knew God so well as did Lucifer. No one, besides the Son, could better make Him known to the inhabitants of heaven and other worlds.

Gradually, imperceptibly to other angels, Lucifer began to entertain doubts about God's goodness and the way He ran His universe. If Lucifer could just get closer to God—actually *be* God, receive the worship of fellow angels—he would be satisfied. The trouble was that Lucifer wanted God's power, not His character. He wanted His privileges without His gracious ways. He wanted His position of authority regardless of the wise and orderly reasons behind it.

So the creature who aspired to be above his own Creator (see 2 Thessalonians 2:4) began to doubt God's character and government, and these doubts, in turn, blossomed into hostility toward God. Insidiously, he proclaimed to angels that God could not be trusted to be fair, honest, unselfish, all-wise, and loving. "He demands you to love Him," he maintained, "because your love gives Him immense satisfaction. Actually, at heart, God is a dictator—arbitrary and vengeful."

God did His best to win the rebel back. He pleaded, He reasoned with him, He loved him, He wept. But Lucifer turned a deaf ear to that gentle voice of love and truth and with a great number of angels revolted against the ever-understanding, generous heart of God.

God could have forced Satan (as Lucifer came to be known) to surrender to Him. He could have destroyed him and his followers by merely leaving them to the natural consequences of their rebellious choice. He could have made them His slaves. But He would not run His universe on the principle of force. Had He blotted out the rebels, the loyal angels would not have understood their destruction to be the natural consequences of evil. They would have pictured God as One who commanded, "Love Me or I'll kill you!" and would have obeyed Him out of fear. But neither fear nor slavery finds a niche in God's way of governing His universe.

Only time and evidence would demonstrate the truth about God and unmask the terrible deceiver.

Chapter 7

# Why Doesn't He Do Something?

"Miss! Miss!"
I glanced toward the direction of the young boy's voice. He was about nine or ten. Quickly, I took in the situation. Evidently, a larger boy, about twelve, had swiped his airplane and was now holding it just out of the younger boy's reach.

"Miss! Will you tell him to give my airplane back to me?"

I paused for a moment and in my imagination I could see myself—a petite, 4'11", 26-year-old woman (who looked closer to 15) shaking her finger at the 12-year-old tormentor (who was taller than she) and commanding, "Look, you thief! Give that airplane back to him! If you don't I'll, I'll—"

Well, what could I do? Join in the chase to try to retrieve the plane? That certainly would not befit my years! I could put on my meanest face, shoot fire out of my dark brown eyes, and try to make his heart quake. And maybe merely my command would be all he would need to make him return the folded piece of paper. Or would it?

A lot of people, like the young boy, are looking to Someone bigger than they are to resolve all their hurts and frustrations by a word. When the boss makes his secretary stay late to do some work he forgot to have her do earlier, how she may wish for God to thunder down to him, "You let her go home!" Or when someone whispers behind our backs, how often we wish He would say, "You gossips, cut that out!"

To some who suffer because of sin, God seems a little small at times for not telling the devil more often, "Stop tempting them; stop hurting them; stop, stop, stop!"

And some ask the question, "Why didn't God tell the devil to stop sinning in the beginning? Could not the Creator who established the heavens and the earth in the beginning control His archenemy? Could He not control us and keep us from sinning by that same power?

Well, of course, some add, we are free to choose. But if we choose to let Him control us, all He would need to do, it seems, is to say the word and our sinfulness would be gone. Like the words of the popular gospel song, "God said it, and I believe it, and that settles it for me," all many of us need for assurance of salvation—and indeed for salvation itself—is God's promise of forgiveness, His declaration of acquittal.

But, if the problem of sin is really the problem of misconceptions about God's character and the resulting distrust of Him, how could God's say-so remedy it?

If we put aside all pretensions of piety and admit that at heart we are a little (if not greatly) afraid of God, does it help us to hear God say, "Fear not, for I am with you. . . . I will up-hold you with My righteous right hand"? Isaiah 41:10, NKJV. Is it comforting to know that someone whom you are afraid of is holding your hand? Especially if that hand is a hundred times more powerful than yours?

Suppose God thundered down from the sky, "Listen! I love you! Now believe it or else!" Would you love Him? Really truly? Fearlessly?

At the foot of Sinai the children of Israel cowed in terror when God thundered out, "I am the Lord your God, who brought you out of the land of Egypt, out of the house of bondage. You shall have no other gods before me." Exodus 20:2, 3, RSV. Even though Moses told the people there was no need to be afraid, they still begged not to have to listen to God's voice themselves.

Their fear did not make them love God more, nor did it keep them from evil. Forty days later they rebelliously chose to worship a lowly beast rather than their majestic Creator.

The story could be repeated throughout history. Fear inevitably leads to rebellious thinking. Perhaps you can remember as a child sitting tensely at your desk after a severe scolding from the teacher. Did you have warm feelings of love and trust? Or did you ever wish you dared to tell your teacher off?

Fear, as used by our gentle God, is only a temporary measure. It is certainly not the primary means of salvation. In fact, fear in and of itself can never save anyone. That is why John wrote, "There is no fear in love, but perfect love casts out fear. For fear has to do with punishment, and he who fears is not perfected in love." 1 John 4:18, RSV.

**The Remedy**

How do you regain the trust in a nation's administrative integrity after Watergate? How do you regain the confidence of a child whose body you have wracked with the pain of your abusive blows and get him to cuddle up in your arms? How do you persuade a former friend whom you've betrayed to confide in you again?

Distrust is rarely unfounded, except in certain types of mental illness. But the root of distrust goes back only to Satan's lies about God. There was no foundation to those lies, only distortions in the darkness.

God calls the problem "sin." And we have a long list of items—outward actions—which we list under that

## WHY DOESN'T HE DO SOMETHING? 35

heading. But these are only the fruit, not the inner problem, misconceptions about God leading to insane distrust.

How do you cure unfounded enmity? How do you regain another's trust lost in you for no reason? These are the questions God has been faced with for centuries—and He has been doing something about it. But the remedy has involved a long, costly process. Only by revealing how He treats sinners for long periods of time and in many situations could God establish the evidence which could alone regain the trust of those who desired to be set free from Satan's lies.

To some it sounds absurd. To many it has seemed too costly. Some consider it the long way around the problem. But to God it is the only way to secure the freedom and peace of the entire universe.

*Chapter 8*

# The Truth Will Set You Free

Experience can be a painful teacher—as well as a false one. We deduce many wrong concepts from a terrifying or awful event in our lives. I think that all my life I shall wrestle with a fear of horses. Why? Partly because of something that happened when I was about thirteen.

My folks decided to buy me a horse. I was excited, yet a little dubious from having fallen off of Shetland ponies while riding bareback. It wasn't easy to bring the colt home; he still wanted to be with his mother, and the traumatic move upset him terribly. After Dad locked him in the barn, he went to get some straw while Toby frantically bucked and whinnied. Hoping to comfort him, I went into his rather small stall. Shutting the door behind me, I suddenly realized that I didn't know where the light was to turn it on. Huddling in a corner near the door, I tried to call out comforting words. But the fear in my voice only made Toby more frantic. Rearing wildly and whinnying in high-pitched fright, Toby's hoofs came down again and again—sometimes only inches from my trembling self. When at last I was able to emerge, I seemed unable to shake off totally my fear of my own horse. As much as I loved him, I was somewhat relieved when a move forced us to sell him.

## THE TRUTH WILL SET YOU FREE 37

If Adam and Eve's fears of God had been born of actual negative encounters with Him, there would be no sinfulness involved. God would be the One at fault. But they chose to believe mere words coming from a glittering serpent, words that were nothing but lies. Hence, though they were deceived, their alienation from God was the result of their own choice. Only by coming once again to perceive the truth about God could their fears (and their sinfulness) be changed to love and trust.

Jesus said to those hoping to destroy His message, "You shall know the truth, and the truth shall make you free." John 8:32, NKJV. If sin were merely a judicial problem and God were primarily a judge, to know the truth about Him would help us very little by way of obtaining the assurance of eternal life. But if sin is an attitude of distrust, fear, and rebellion toward God and is based on lies about His character, knowing the truth about Him is the essence of salvation. After all, one need not be afraid to face a God who has always been gracious.

Perhaps, though, the question remains; "What precisely are the lies about God which led to man's fall?"

A close look at the implications of the serpent's utterances recorded in Genesis 3 reveals the following false concepts of God:

1. Isn't God being too particular in withholding this tree from you?
2. Isn't His command arbitrary?
3. God is selfish.
4. You will not die!
5. God doesn't always mean what He says.
6. He has lied to you.
7. The fruit won't hurt you; if God fulfills His threat, He will have to kill you.
8. God asks you to surrender everything to Him, but actually to eat of this tree would make you equal with Him.

9. He is hiding the fact that if you ate this fruit, you would become like Him in wisdom and power.
10. He is afraid you will usurp His authority.
11. He is trying to protect Himself.
12. You cannot really know God unless you are a god.
13. God does not value beauty nor does He want you to enjoy lovely food.

If you were God, faced with a list of charges such as this, what would you do? How would you go about providing Adam and Eve with evidence that you were not what Satan claimed you were? Especially when, as you came to talk to them, they ran from you in terror?

Deception does terrible things to the mind. Belief in a false picture of God has led to insane actions ranging from persecution and immorality to suicide. Once a lie is believed to be the truth it so damages the mind that real truth can scarcely gain an entrance.

Nevertheless, not everyone in the universe believed Satan's charges. God had many intelligent beings who refused to swallow the claims of the Deceiver. Yet even the loyal angels had lingering questions. What was God really like? So, for their sakes, God determined to reveal to them that He was not as Satan had made Him out to be—tyrannical, selfish, vengeful, unforgiving, and unbending. In the process, the same evidence that would confirm the loyal ones in their trust of God would win some of His now rebellious children back to Him.

The story of the evidence is the story of all sixty-six books of the Bible. In this inspired record, we find recounted the history of God's dealings with us sinners. We can see the way He has dealt with sin so as to show that it is not His fault. We see the outlines of the truth about Him.

Sometimes we wish the Book were not a record, but a collection of statements or rules. Why then did God reveal Himself this way? Because mere claims do not prove anything. Rules are only the first-aid methods God has used to protect us in our immaturity from destroying ourselves. Neither rules or claims give us complete assurance that we can trust God, but a record of His dealings with human beings gives us a convincing picture of His character of love.

*Chapter 9*

# The God of the Bible

Picture yourself as a new teacher of a fifth-grade classroom full of undisciplined students. The previous teacher lasted six weeks. The one before her managed barely for one semester. The school was closed before that because no one could restore order. Now it is your turn.

Already, as you survey your motley group, you can see signs of simmering rebellion. Peter already has yanked Sally's long straight hair, and the latter is sobbing with her head down on her desk. Jim, the hyperactive one (or are they all hyperactive?) repeatedly bangs a book violently on the desk, stopping only to jump on his chair and perform his favorite act. Mary shouts obscenities at Ruth, who is about to slug her jaw. Under your desk you catch Shane crawling toward your foot with a rubber band poised to spring toward your ankle. The rest of the twenty-five children are clustered in small groups, loudly discussing what they will do to you.

No doubt you are wondering, "How will I restore order so that they can begin to learn something?"

That has been God's question throughout history, particularly during Old Testament times.

We too often blame some of the mind-shuddering stories in the Old Testament on a bad god, or at least a bad picture of God. Surely He didn't really drown most of the

## THE GOD OF THE BIBLE 41

world in a flood, destroy Sodom and Gomorrah with fire, order Sabbath-breakers and adulterers to be stoned, destroy Uzzah for touching the ark, bury Korah, Dathan, and Abiram alive and burn up their innocent children. Laid end to end and read superficially, apart from the whole of the Bible, they leave a very distorted picture of our heavenly Father. In the light of Satan's charge that He is a tyrant, how could God's strong measures do anything to prove His enemy wrong? It appears, at first sight, that it is God—not sin—which destroys sinners. Thus His commands are merely arbitrary injunctions made by a selfish God. If sin didn't naturally lead to death, what could be wrong with it? At a glance, the Old Testament stories seem to do a bad job of demonstrating the truth about God.

Yet when the Bible is read as a whole in light of the controversy between God and Satan, the picture becomes clear. The stories weave together into a perfect whole. We begin to understand that, as in our imaginary story above, God has been faced with extremely rebellious children. Children who would not respect a deity who did not use force. Children who were stiff-necked, hardheaded, and often unwilling to listen.

Standing back, as it were, reading through the entire Book, one captures the heart-rending agony of a very loving, friendly God who tries—and frequently fails—to win His prodigal family to come home. He tries first one measure, and then another. If thundering from Sinai is the only thing that will enable them to listen, He will thunder. If painful amputation of Israelites is necessary in order to check the destructive rebellion spreading through Israel, God will perform the necessary surgery. If they must have rules spelled out for the sake of their low understanding, He will stoop to list the rules.

In the Old Testament, we find our God doing all of the above. Time after time, He ran after them in the form of prophets crying, "Why will you die, O house of Israel? For I have no pleasure in the death of any one, says the Lord God; so turn, and live." Ezekiel 18:31, 32, RSV. As though He Himself were responsible for the people's behavior, He pleaded through Micah, "O my people, what have I done to you? In what have I wearied you? Answer me!" Micah 6:3, RSV. To a wandering Israel, determined to reject His gracious ways, He sobbed, "How can I give you up, Ephraim, how surrender you, Israel?" Hosea 11:8, NEB.

The theme runs through the entire Bible. Understanding that theme and God's attempts to keep in touch with His rebellious, wandering people, we can find a consistant picture all the way through. Against that picture we can better understand what salvation is all about.

For, you see, salvation is not a legal document, nor a receipt of purchase, nor an act of appeasement, nor an escape route from hell, nor a ritual of cleansing, nor the cessation of God's wrath.

Salvation is a story. A story about God. Our participation involves how we decide to read it.

## Teacher of the Universe

Recently a couple of friends and I discussed what role God would have assumed were He to come in modern times. The possibilities are endless. Would He be a physician? A contractor? A computer programmer? A manufacturer? A businessman? A musician? A newsreporter? An engineer? A farmer? A minister?

While we explored the various roles, I suddenly realized something very important. He might assume any of the above occupations, but regardless of what He did He would also be a teacher.

Now, for God to be a teacher is nothing new. God has always been teaching—but not in an ordinary classroom nor with ordinary methods. He taught the intelligent beings of the universe while creating this world. Throughout the history of the sin problem everything He has done has formed a part of the truth about Himself which He has sought to teach the universe—including us. So, when God came to our world, He simply carried on His teaching process as a man.

One by one, He refuted Satan's lies with the evidence of His life. Although He was the Creator of the universe, He worked for twenty-five years with wood which He could have spoken into existence. He never owned His own home, He often depended on others for his very food, and at times He overworked Himself in tireless, caring ministry for others.

He was a physician without pay. Multitudes flocked to Him to be healed. He ate with sinners and outcasts. Most of all, He taught the people about His heavenly Father.

"You want to know what my kingdom is like?" He asked. "Watch Me, listen, study. As you see Me, so you see My Father. The way I act is the way I choose to run My universe." God has always used the demonstration of truth as His chosen method of teaching. Understanding and learning take place best by observation. Furthermore, only consistent demonstrated evidence can restore and confirm trust. So Jesus' life on earth was the climax of all God has done to *show* His intelligent creatures what He is like. See Hebrews 1:1, 2.

In the end the message came through clearly to the universe. God was not arbitrary, vengeful, unbending, or cruel; God was a Friend. How He must have disliked having to thunder from Sinai to get them to listen. How He must have abhorred the stonings, the flood, the burning of Sodom! Teacher that He is, God taught His loyal friends to understand fully what He was like. *Understand,* because the essence of true learning is understanding. God will have no programmed robots in His universe.

But what about our salvation? Didn't God come as a Saviour? Of course, He did. But the best definition of *saviour* is "physician." Since sin happens in the mind, to save us from it requires healing of the mind. Only God can heal all the warped thinking and resulting bad behavior resulting from our acceptance of Satan's lies. But *how* He prefers to heal us involves inviting us to see the evidence that He is not what Satan portrayed Him as being. It has to do with the story, God's way of teaching.

If we reach out to Him through His Word, He will teach us the truth about Himself—the truth that we can trust Him, the truth that He is a freedom-giving, gracious God.

As we respond in trust, we will have assurance—about God.

Chapter 10

# Assurance Before God's Judgment Bar

The bumper sticker jumped at me with bold letters. Slowing in the parking lot, I turned back for another look. Yes, I had read it correctly: "Without Jesus, you don't have a prayer."

On the way home I thought about those words. What did they mean? Did they mean, if Jesus were not continually praying for us, God would not hear our prayers? Is the prayer of one who fails to pray "in Jesus' name" thrown out of heaven?

Is God the Father reluctant to love us and answer our prayers? Must Jesus constantly pour soothing oil on troubled waters coming from God's throne?

One of the biggest threats to our ability to trust God is the belief that God is somehow less loving and merciful than His Son. Because Jesus was born a baby, grew up as a child, and walked the earth as a man, we find it easier to believe that He is truly "on our side." He is the meek and lowly One, upon whose lap even the most timid child eagerly sat. So Jesus is viewed as more approachable than God, because He is human as well as divine (which suggests that humanity is more merciful than divinity!).

Are we kinder than God?

Jesus gave the opposite picture of His Father. Turning to the fathers in His audience, He asked them, "Would you give your son a stone when he asked you for bread? What father," He said, "would do this?" See Matthew 7:9. Then He gave the punchline: "If you then, who are evil, know how to give good gifts to your children, how much more will your Father who is in heaven give good things to those who ask him!" Matthew 7:11, RSV.

Lest we think such a statement must be confined to the New Testament, Isaiah records similar words. "Can a woman forget her own baby and not love the child she bore? Even if a mother should forget her child, I will never forget you." Isaiah 49:15, TEV.

If we believe the words of Jesus, He assures us that "He who has seen me has seen the Father." John 14:9, RSV. His life alone demonstrates that God is on our side.

How did Jesus treat sinners? He ate with them and stayed in their homes. To a woman caught in adultery, He said gently, "Neither do I condemn you. . . . Go now and leave your life of sin." John 8:11, NIV. He had compassion on those who were considered condemned by God. Never did He set up a judgment bar before which He arraigns contrite sinners.

By the end of His ministry, His disciples were confused. They had been looking for a conqueror to free their nation from Roman oppression. From time to time they had argued among themselves as to who would be "first" or "greatest" in the new kingdom. They even expected their Messiah to turn Judge to condemn all sinners in the earth. But throughout His ministry nothing of the kind had happened. Then, to top it all off, Jesus tied a servant's towel around His waist and washed their dirty feet.

So consumed were they with the idea of a powerful kingdom, that they little comprehended His last message about the Father: "Though I have been speaking figuratively, a time is coming when I will no longer use this kind of language but will tell you plainly about my Father. In that day you will ask in my name. *I am not saying that I will ask the Father on your behalf. No, the Father himself loves you.* John 16:25-27, NIV, emphasis supplied.

God the Father is just as compassionate as His Son. Paul's major point in Romans is that all three Members of the Godhead—Father, Son, and Holy Spirit—are equally gracious; they are all on our side. See Romans 8.

## Someone in Between

As a child, did you ever damage something in a neighbor's yard while playing with your friends—only to have your mother (or father) make you go over and apologize? Did you ever wish your parents would say the "I'm sorry" for you? Or have you ever longed for someone to plead on your behalf, so that the anger of the injured party simmered down by the time you had to face them? Or, that someone would be a go-between?

Due to our acceptance of Satan's lies, we often have the same feelings about facing God in the judgment. We want an intermediary to stand between us and the "wrathful" Father. Someone to hide our ugly sinfulness from His holy eyes. Someone to plead in our behalf.

Originally, God talked face to face with Adam and Eve. But, after they began to believe Satan's lies, they ran in terror from their friendly God, when He came to visit them in the garden. As a result God mercifully sent angels to communicate with them and their descendents. Yet, occasionally He found friends such as Abraham, Job, and Moses with whom He could talk "face to face, as a man speaks to his friend." Exodus 33:11, RSV. To others God had to communicate "in dark speech." Numbers 12:8, RSV.

It was not until Israel camped at the foot of Sinai, that a mediator—someone in between—was first requested.

And the request came from the people, not from God. When the people heard God thunder from the mountain, they were so frightened that they begged Moses to do the speaking. "Do not have God speak to us," they told Moses, "or we will die."Exodus 20:19, NIV. Later, when reminding the people of this event, Moses said, "At that time I stood between the Lord and you to declare to you the word of the Lord, because you were afraid of the fire." Deuteronomy 5:5, NIV.

Has God ever wanted anyone between Himself and us?

To have a mediator was not God's original plan. He would rather speak to us personally. Indeed, we need no one between us and Himself. Yet, if we are too afraid of Him, He will meet us where we are. That is one of the reasons Jesus came—so that we could have a three-and-a-half-year taste of basking in God's presence *comfortably* with no one in between.

## The Accuser

There is something ominous about seeing a flashing red light in your rearview mirror. By the time you have pulled off the road, your mind has gone through mental gymnastics in an effort to assess what you've done wrong. Sometimes you draw a blank, but sometimes you know!

Sometimes highway patrolmen are kind and understanding, at other times you drive away with a slimmer checking account, but one thing is certain, you understand that he was right and you are wrong. But there are still other times when you aren't sure you are wrong, and you grope around for some means of defense, like the evening a slightly tipsy city policeman threatened to give me a ticket for a light that had just burned out, of which I wasn't aware as yet.

Sometimes we sense that someone or something in this vast universe is somewhat like an unfair policeman.

Someone or something must be accusing us. If this is not the case, our conscience is doing a good job of berating us. In the end we frequently decide that God is the One who is accusing us. After all, who else could be doing this? And who else would do such an accurate job?

Yet the Bible tells us the opposite about God. As we noticed above, Jesus is God and He did not come to condemn the world, but to save it. See John 3:17. Paul asks, "Who will bring any charge against those whom God has chosen? It is God who justifies. Who is he that condemns?" Romans 8:33, 34, NIV.

If nothing else, is there anyone to accuse us? Yes, there is. John, in the Revelation, calls him "the one who stood before our God and accused our brothers day and night." Revelation 12:10, TEV. In Zechariah, he is known as Satan, God's enemy. Here we see him arguing strongly against God's people. "Then he [an angel] showed me Joshua the high priest [representing God's people] standing before the angel of the Lord, and Satan standing at his right side to accuse him." Zechariah 3:1, RSV. In Job, Satan accuses this faithful worshiper of God before the angels.

Just as Satan has accused God before the entire universe, so he now seeks to accuse us. No longer can he flaunt his lies about God in the faces of the loyal angels, for God won His case at the cross. But what about us? With our past records, do angels and others in God's universe have evidence that they can trust us to be comfortable to live with for eternity?

In the freedom with which God runs this universe, He would never command angels arbitrarily to put up with us. Just as He offered to demonstrate the trustworthiness of Job before them in the face of Satan's charges, so He offers to show them the evidence that we would make good citizens of heaven.

When Satan accuses us before the universe, he reminds

all onlookers of our sins, our acceptance of his lies, our misrepresentations of God. While God well knows the record of our past, He also knows that we have come to know Him and have been won back to trust and love. To this He points as the evidence that we can be trusted with eternal life. That is why Paul said that faith is the righteousness God requires. See Romans 4:5, 9.

Thus the real question in the judgment is not, What does God think of us? God has always thought of us in the same way the father thought about his prodigal son in Jesus' parable. The greatest concern of the universe is, rather, What do we think of God? Have we come to love and trust Him?

**The Evidence of Our Trust**

As a child, I idolized my older brother. Nearly everything he did I tried to copy, until my mother despaired of ever teaching me to be a "young lady" instead of a tomboy! I hammered nails, played with Tonka trucks instead of dolls, and became a favorite in the little boys' softball games. I was very proud when he gave me *his* castoff mitt, *his* erector set, and *his* old saw.

Actually, I fulfilled an old psychological law that Paul talks about. "We all, with unveiled face, beholding the glory of the Lord, are being changed into his likeness from one degree of glory to another." 2 Corinthians 3:18, RSV. Since *glory* stands for *character*, this simply means that we become like the One we worship and admire. It is an inevitable process, or natural law.

The greatest evidence that we have rejected Satan's lies and have accepted Jesus' picture of God is how we reflect by our treatment of others the way God treats us. "We know that we have passed from death to life," John wrote, "because we love our brothers. Anyone who does not love remains in death." 1 John 3:14, NIV.

It is this evidence of our changed lives that Jesus presents before the universe. In the end, as He put it while on earth, it is not the Father or Himself who will be our Judge but the truth which will testify for or against us. See John 5:22; 12:48. That is, we are judged by the truth. For God can save only those who have put truth above all else in their lives—and will do so forever.

No one would be comfortable living in God's presence who did not possess the ability to love others and who did not love God. God is love in His very essence. His law is love. The universe is operated on love, freedom, and truth. No one is forced to change. No one is forced to know God. What an assurance of eternal life this gives us!

There are some who wish God didn't allow us so much freedom. Why doesn't He protect us more? Why didn't He make it impossible for us to sin? Why couldn't He arbitrarily change us so we would be happy in heaven?

But these questions themselves imply that God should be a little like Satan's claims in order to "save us." However, could you trust a God who would change you without your cooperation? How could you trust such a God not to make you a turtle someday instead of a human being? Could you genuinely trust a God who simply programmed you to trust Him? Would your trust reflect the idea that God could be trusted, or would it reflect the fact that you had simply been manipulated?

There can be no genuine love and trust and joy without freedom. Freedom means that we are responsible for our own choices. Freedom means that we are not mere products of our environment or victims of impossible-to-be-changed habits. We are free—free to worship the true God or the god of Satan's lies; free to decide whether or not we are saved.

At the same time, God will do all He can to save us, short of forcing our wills. He will run after us again and again. He will pour out His love on us and seek to reveal

Himself to us in His Word. And He will do His best to defend us in the judgment. But He will never force us.

Force only leads to fear. And where there is fear there is no assurance of any kind. The way God presides in the judgment can give us the assurance that He absolutely will not run His universe on fear.

*Chapter 11*

# A Swordless God

Sometimes we pity the forefathers of modern America. Think of what they lacked in the way of entertainment! No sports. No amusement parks. No computers. No table games. No television. They worked from sunup to sundown. The word *entertainment* in Webster's original dictionary did not mean what it means now.

Yet, we need not think of them as totally deprived of what one would consider entertainment. During periods of religious revival they had tremendous entertainment. Preachers swayed back and forth on stage while describing vividly the terrors of hell to poor lost sinners. Hotter and hotter grew the story (and likewise the meeting house) until the listeners thought they could hear the very flames crackling around them and see their livid glow. Men groaned with anguish; women screamed and fainted; some rolled on the ground; others swayed back and forth like reeds in a hurricane. In panic, many were "converted," but one could not be sure that their minds remained sane.

But that was the style in certain places during the early nineteenth century. People loved to participate in such dramatic diversions from the hard toil of everyday life. The drama was compelling; for what could be better than a mad god glowering over his sinful victims of wrath as they writhed screaming on molten waves? The famous piercing eyes of Charles Finney, a notable revivalist, are said to have conveyed a convincing picture of such a deity.

What few of those participants knew was that such a drama was created by Satan, not by God. Its source lay in Satan's lie to Eve, "You will not die." For centuries the arch deceiver has worked on that lie. In spite of the fact that God clearly withheld immortality from our first parents until they had been tested and proved loyal (see Genesis 3:19, 22, 23), Satan persuaded their descendants to believe that the "soul" of man had been created immortal. And, of course, if the souls of the wicked lived forever, what would a loveless God do with them? The archenemy of God devised an answer to his own question—the popular concept of hell.

The Bible teaches no such concept. Rather, it teaches that the wages of sin is death. See Romans 6:23. God alone has immortality. See 1 Timothy 6:16. Jesus Himself likened death to a sleep from which one would awaken. John 11:11. Furthermore, no truly loving God would torture even His most erring children throughout eternity. All will perish completely.

But the question remains: How? Will God finally lose patience and kill the wicked?

For many no question is so crucial as this one. If God arbitrarily kills the wicked at the end, whether in eternal hell fire or in some other kind of summary execution, then we are under the threat of a swinging sword. If sin in itself does not naturally lead to the final death of the sinner, some will conclude that there is nothing ultimately wrong with sin except that an offended God says so. According to this line of reasoning, God is the final destroyer, not sin. He, not sin, is our great enemy.

If, for example, doctors killed every victim of cancer,

which would we fear, the disease or the doctors? We would fear the physicians, would we not? Thus the issue meets us unequivocally at these crossroads: What should we fear—sin or God?

## The Cross Is the Answer

At the foundation of all erroneous views of assurance is the belief that God has said, "Love me or I'll kill you." The response to that kind of God could hardly be called love. The escape from sin has too frequently been misunderstood as merely an escape from hell, but it is much more than this. It involves the peace coming from victory over sin in this life as well as escape from the ultimate result of sin, which is eternal separation from God, the source of life, in other words, eternal death. As a result of this misunderstanding many have misinterpreted Matthew 1:21 to mean that Jesus "shall save his people from the wrath of an offended God" rather than, Jesus "will save his people from their sins." RSV.

Jesus came to do the latter, not the former. His death is rightly called the "at-one-ment"—the reconciliation of man to God. More than anything else, Christ's death answers the question: "Does sin result in death?"

We are not talking here primarily of the first death, but of the second death—the wages of sin, not its natural result in this life. Who causes this death?

Before the witnessing universe of loyal and evil angels God demonstrated through His Son's death the answer to that question. In Gethsemane and on the cross Jesus experienced the awful separation that the sinner will face in the final punishment of the wicked. Some have referred to this experience as suffering the wrath of God.

Does this mean that God was angry, and because of His anger, He put Jesus to death? Never! Sin by its very nature brings about a separation between Christ and His Father. This is why He cried out, "My God, my God, why hast thou forsaken me?" Matthew 27:46. This is the separation the sinner will feel. In the case of the lost it is the natural result of their choice. So, although the Bible does speak of the wrath of God, it is not wrath as commonly understood.

When Paul describes God's wrath "against all ungodliness and wickedness of men" (Romans 1:18, RSV), he emphasizes that it is simply God giving up sinners to their own sinful choice. Three times in the same chapter he says, "God gave them up." In Romans 4:25 he states explicitly that Jesus also was "given up."*

What does this mean?

When we stand at the foot of the crosss, do we have any evidence that God destroyed His Son? On the contrary, as we listen we can hear His anguished cry, "My God, my God, why hast thou forsaken me?" Mark 15:34, RSV. If God really did torture Jesus, the words would have been significantly different. There is no evidence from the entire New Testament that God even touched or spoke to His Son. He simply "gave Him up" as He will finally give up sinners. Made to be sin though He knew no sin (see 2 Corinthians 5:21), Jesus died as a result of the consequences of taking upon Him the sin of the world.

God's loyal, intelligent beings understood completely what the cross meant. Satan's lies that God would finally destroy sinners had been met face to face and vanquished in the one act. It was clearly shown that there never had been any need to be afraid of an angry god in the judgment. God had never said, "Love me or I'll kill you."

---

*Some translations render this verse incorrectly, conveying the idea that Jesus was put to death. But the original Greek word literally reads "was given up."

The warning given to Adam and Eve not to eat of the tree was not an arbitrary command, "Don't eat of it or I'll destroy you." Rather for them to go near the tree was to encounter the "father of lies" whose words, if accepted, would bring death.

## The Final Wrath

If, by His death, Jesus showed that sin—not God—would finally destroy sinners, what about the many references to consuming fire in the Bible? No fire destroyed Jesus at the cross; does His death really clarify the issue at stake?

Merely reading about "the lake of fire" (Revelation 20:14) and "torment" in "fire and brimstone" (Revelation 14:10, 11), tempt many to answer this question negatively. But a close look at the biblical evidence reveals the real answer.

Paul wrote, "Our God is a consuming fire." Hebrews 12:29. Before sin entered the mind of Lucifer (or "light bearer," as some translations render Isaiah 14:12), this mighty angel walked amid the stones of fire in God's presence. See Ezekiel 28:16. More specifically, the Israelites saw God's *glory* like a devouring fire on the top of Mount Sinai (Exodus 24:17). What is His glory?

*Glory* in the Bible serves to denote both character and a kind of radiance. God's glory is both His actual physical radiance and the kind of Person He is. Originally His glory bathed Adam and Eve in a life-giving glow. Angels feel most comfortable living in His presence.

In Isaiah 33:14 the question is asked, "Who among us shall dwell with the devouring fire? who among us shall dwell with everlasting burning?" Satan would have us believe that those who reject God's offer of salvation will, but the Bible says that those who dwell with everlasting fire are those who walk "righteously." Verse 15.

To those who cling to Satan's lies and their destructive results, God's glory is a consuming fire. Sin has so changed them that, if surrounded by the presence of their gracious God, they will be destroyed by the life-giving radiance of love.

In mercy God has held His self-giving light back from us sinners. As a Man He clothed Himself in human flesh, thus hiding His glory, so that we might come to know Him and be unafraid. The disciples felt at ease in His presence; consequently they could scarcely comprehend that they were such close friends of *God*. But Jesus explicitly told them, "He who has seen me has seen the Father." John 14:9, RSV.

Those who study and accept Jesus' picture of God will someday be able to stand unafraid in His presence. Those, on the other hand, who cling to Satan's lies will find sin the destructive agent to cause their eternal death.

At the crux of the matter, we need to fear only one thing: that we will reject the remedy—the good news about God. And if we have accepted it and continue to study to know Him better in His Word, we will not be afraid of anything. For when we know we can trust God, our quest for assurance is at an end.

Chapter 12

# Coming to Know God

### How Much Time Do I Have?

As children most of us played hide-and-seek, that rather ancient game invented to wear out hyperactive children. While one of us covered our eyes and counted, the rest of our playmates ran off to hide. I can remember some of those times as I buried my eyes in my hands by the old English walnut tree and counted 1, 2, 3, 4, 5, 6, 7, 8, 9, 10 . . . as fast as I could until I reached 100. Then with a triumphant but ominous yell, designed to stop everyone's breathing, I would shout, "Here I come, ready or not!"

We no longer play this game with our friends. Our years of maturity only make us smile at the memories. But unfortunately, many of us have never stopped playing it with God. We picture our infinite Creator with a stopwatch in one hand and a gavel in the other. With one eye He watches the hands of the watch; with the other He studies the earth. Soon (we have no real idea when) He will snap the stem of the watch down and shout, "Here I come, ready or not!" And having descended from heaven, He will take home all those who happen to be ready at the moment. The rest will be lost.

Like the children's game, this idea has often been thought to be quite effective in wearing out hyperactive Christians so they will settle down enough to be ready for the second coming.

But, in fact, it has given us only more anxiety and fear. Surely, in light of the truth about God revealed by Jesus, we know that God will never set an arbitrary date in an effort purposefully to surprise us. To His disciples—and to us—Jesus gave a list of signs to prepare us to know when His coming was near. One of those signs (Matthew 24:14) was that the good news about His Father will go to all the world before the end.

This fits in with Peter's concept of God in writing about the delay of Christ's return. "It is not that the Lord is slow in fulfilling his promise, as some suppose, but that he is very patient with you, because it is not his will for any to be lost, but for all to come to repentance." 2 Peter 3:9, NEB. Obviously, God is more concerned with saving as many as He can than with some arbitrary timetable for getting rid of sinners.

So we can trust God to do His best to save us—why not give ourselves the time needed to come to know Him? This does not mean we can safely while away our time, ignoring His gracious offer. Not at all. As we said earlier, sin affects the mind, and the longer we put off taking the remedy, the greater the damage we do to ourselves. It is possible to become so hardened toward the truth about God that we find it virtually impossible to perceive it. We might even come to the point where we don't want to know God.

Should we take this course, our Great Physician would be terribly grieved, but not angry, with us for rejecting His offer to heal us. He would never torture us in punishment for not coming to Him. Had the prodigal never returned home, the Father would not have come after him with a club. Had he lay dying in the pigpen, the Father would not have come to beat him until he died. He would have cried, that's all.

With such a gracious God as this to trust, surely we will wish to so know Him that we can have the assurance that He is the way Jesus—not Satan—has pictured Him. The real urgency is not the shortness of earth's future or even our own liabilities, but rather that God is worth getting to know! In light of what He is really like, our greatest desire will be to know Him better.

## How to Know Him Better

It is through the Bible that God has endeavored to make Himself known to us. But tragically, this Book has been so misunderstood and misinterpreted that many find its God totally unattractive. Just a look at the many different conceptions of God in the various denominations tells us that either He cannot be truly known, or that few understand how to read His book.

So the question remains, "How does one read the Bible?"

Many answers have been given to this question. Thousands of books have been written with detailed "how to" instructions. Some of the methodologies are so complex as to be beyond comprehension. However the Bible answer is simple by comparison. It is so simple that a child can understand it. If the Bible's purpose is to reveal God to us, then as we read, we need ask only one logical question: What does this chapter, this verse, this story tell me about God? Or, more broadly: What contribution does this section of the Bible make to the picture of God in the entire Bible?

Only one rule is needed beyond this. No one story or verse or passage is more important than the rest of the Bible. Nothing should be lifted from its immediate context and the whole of all other books. Sometimes one may not find the key to a puzzling story until he reads another book or the Bible as a whole.

Another help is to get hold of a good modern translation, one that is easy to read. Most of these may be obtained through your nearest Christian bookstore. The New Testament was originally written in the common Greek spoken in those days by the "man on the street." Certainly God is not offended if we read His Word in a language commonly spoken in our day!

Above all else, remember that God is eager to reveal Himself to you. He has promised to send His Spirit of truth specifically to teach us concerning the truth about Himself. While at first, we may have some difficulties with Satan's lies and our own false presuppositions, we will find that continuous, daily study provides us with solid evidences of the truth about God.

There is no shortcut to persistent study of the Bible. The healing God provides does not take place in an instant. As in the case of many physical medications, we must "take" the entire bottle in regular small doses.

## Does It Work?

Does this understanding of God really provide one with the assurance that he has eternal life? It certainly can, if we are willing.

In His prayer to His Father just before His crucifixion, Jesus said, "This is eternal life, that they know thee the only true God, and Jesus Christ whom thou hast sent." John 17:3, RSV.

Do you have the assurance that you know God? On what basis could you say Yes? Nearly every religion claims to have "the truth" about God. Within Christianity, there are many different conceptions of Him, nearly all of which differ with the one explained here. How can we know?

Perhaps the only way is to read and study the Bible so thoroughly that we actually can "know that we know" God. With the aid of the Spirit, this can take place rather quickly. After all, God has not spent the last 6,000 years hiding the evidences of the truth from us! Rather He has been seeking to reveal them.

This means of assurance is not as tangible and easily defined, perhaps, as buying a ticket to heaven or hearing a legal sentence or simply saying, "I accept Christ." But it can be far more reassuring.

You see, with this picture of God, I'm not afraid of the One who is coming to pick me up at the airport. I don't crave or fear a legal verdict, because I see Him as a Father, not as a Judge. And I understand what it means to say, "I accept Christ." It means I have studied Jesus' picture of His Father, and I like it. I like it so much that I want to be like Him. I accept what He portrays as truth for my head and heart. Futhermore, it means that I have an already gracious Father-God who will do all He can to save me.

Most of all, it means that I can intelligently trust God. I don't have to trust something inferior to my Creator, such as blood or grace or a Son who persuades a reluctant Father or who offers His life to Him as a means of appeasement or a packaged gift or a cross or my own faith. I don't have to try to trust God as though He were not worthy of my trust.

No, I can trust Him because He is trustworthy. And I can trust Him, even if I should let Him down and be lost. For I know He would not torture me as He gave me up; but He would cry over me as He cried over Israel, "How can I give you up?" He would miss me throughout eternity.

Because I know and trust Him, I'm not afraid of God any more. I am not afraid of Him, regardless of which decision I make. What freedom this brings me! What a desire it gives me to be saved, to be sure not to miss out on such a beautiful relationship and intelligent understanding which will grow forever.

In short, my assurance is not that *I* am saved but that *God* is a Friend I can trust.